The Best of C. L. Aldridge
Mandalas

Extraordinary Coloring Books for Extraordinary People

"No one is useless
in this world who
lightens the burdens
of another."

—Charles Dickens

Also by C. L. Aldridge

Flowers and Dreams
A Coloring Book of Beautiful Botanical Symmetry

Adult Coloring Book of Flower Inspirations
Beautiful Floral Patterns, Botanical Mandalas, Gemstones, Lovely Words and More!

Flowers and Flyers
Adult Coloring Book of Flowers, Songbirds, Hummingbirds, Butterflies, Owls, Ornamentals and More!

Travel Size Book of Flowers, Birds Butterflies and More!
Your Coloring Book for the Road.
(Measures 6" x 9", just the right size to tuck in a purse, a travel bag or a desk drawer.)

Flowers and Whimsy
Adult Coloring Book of Fun to Color Ornamental Floral Patterns, Whimsical Butterflies, Dragonflies and More!

Flowers of Fantasy
A Coloring Book of Fantastical Floral Designs

Flowers of Wonder
A Coloring Book of Fabulous Fantasy Flowers

Fantasy Flower Garden
Adult Coloring book of Fantastic Flowers and Friendly Animals

Fabulous Flowers
A Coloring book of Flowers, Imagination and Symmetry

The Best of C. L. Aldridge Coloring Books: Fan Favorites
Adult Coloring book of Fantastic Flowers, Symmetry and Design

This book is dedicated to the fabulous fans of my work, whether they have been with me since the very beginning or are just now discovering my work. I wouldn't want to do this job without you! Thank you for breathing life into my drawing with your colors!

* * * * *

IMPORTANT INFORMATION FOR USING THIS BOOK

- This book contains 48 original design hand-drawn illustrations to color. Each page is printed SINGLE SIDED (back is blank).

- The pages are printed on #60 lb bright white paper which performs well for all brands of colored pencils and crayons, without the need of a blotter page.

- To avoid any "Uh Oh's" and the associated disappointment, **Marker and Gel Pen and/or Water Medium users are STRONGLY ENCOURAGED to USE A BLOTTER SHEET** behind the drawing to avoid any possibility of bleed through to the next page. Several blank blotter and color testing pages are provided at the end of this book.

- Most IMPORTANT of all: Relax, have fun, stand-up and stretch often, and remember that sometimes the most beautiful things come from what we think at first are mistakes, but which turn out to be art's way of working magic!

This Book Belongs To:

_____

_____

_____

Date:_____

© 2019 C. L. Aldridge

© 2019 C. L. Aldridge

© 2019 C. L. Aldridge

© 2019 C. L. Aldridge

© 2019 C. L. Aldridge

© 2019 C. L. Aldridge

© 2019 C. L. Aldridge

© 2019 C. L. Aldridge

© 2019 C. L. Aldridge

© 2019 C. L. Aldridge

© 2019 C. L. Aldridge

© 2019 C. L. Aldridge

© 2019 C. L. Aldridge

© 2019 C. L. Aldridge

© 2019 C. L. Aldridge

© 2019 C. L. Aldridge

"No one is useless in this world who lightens the burdens of another."

~Charles Dickens

© 2019 C. L. Aldridge

© 2019 C. L. Aldridge

© 2019 C. L. Aldridge

© 2019 C. L. Aldridge

© 2019 C. L. Aldridge

© 2019 C. L. Aldridge

© 2019 C. L. Aldridge

© 2019 C. L. Aldridge

This page is intentionally left blank as a
place for you to test out your coloring mediums
and/or to tear out and use as a blotter page.

This page is intentionally left blank as a
place for you to test out your coloring mediums
and/or to tear out and use as a blotter page.

Extraordinary Coloring Books for Extraordinary People

Available in Print at Amazon.com Worldwide
Full Books and Individual pages PDF's as Instant
downloads at CLAldridgeArt on Etsy.com

@ www.Etsy.com/shop/CLAldridgeArt